Morning Meals
Around the World

by **Maryellen Gregoire**

illustrated by **Jeff Yesh**

Thanks to our advisers for their
expertise, research, and advice:

JoAnne Buggey, Ph.D., Elementary Social Studies
College of Education and Human Development
University of Minnesota, Minneapolis
Member, National Council for the Social Studies

Susan Kesselring, M.A., Literacy Educator
Rosemount-Apple Valley-Eagan (Minnesota) School District

PICTURE WINDOW BOOKS
Minneapolis, Minnesota

The editor wishes to thank Susanne Mattison, Culinary Specialist for Byerly's, for her expert advice on preparing the recipes for this book.

Managing Editor: Bob Temple
Creative Director: Terri Foley
Editor: Sara E. Hoffmann
Editorial Adviser: Andrea Cascardi
Copy Editor: Laurie Kahn
Designer: Nathan Gassman
Page production: Picture Window Books
The illustrations in this book were rendered digitally.

Picture Window Books
1710 Roe Crest Drive
North Mankato, MN 56003
1-877-845-8392
www.capstonepub.com

Library of Congress Cataloging-in-Publication Data
Gregoire, Maryellen.
Morning meals around the world / by Maryellen Gregoire ;
illustrated by Jeff Yesh.
p. cm. — (Meals around the world)
Summary: Discusses the variety of foods people around the
world might have for breakfast.
ISBN 13: 978-1-4048-0280-3 (hardcover)
ISBN 13: 978-1-4048-1130-0 (paperback)
1. Breakfasts—Juvenile literature. 2. Cookery, International—
Juvenile literature.
[1. Breakfasts. 2. Food habits.] I. Yesh, Jeff, 1971- ill. II. Title. III.
Series.
TX733.G75 2004
641.5'2—dc22   2003016450

Yawn and stretch. It's time to wake up.
Do you smell something good to eat?

Your morning meal is important because
it gives you energy to start your day.
All around the world, people start the
day with delicious food and drinks.

NORTH
AMERICA

UNITED STATES
pages 6-7

MEXICO
pages 14-15

NICARAGUA
pages 16-17

SOUTH
AMERICA

What are they eating and drinking?
Let's travel around the world and
find out!

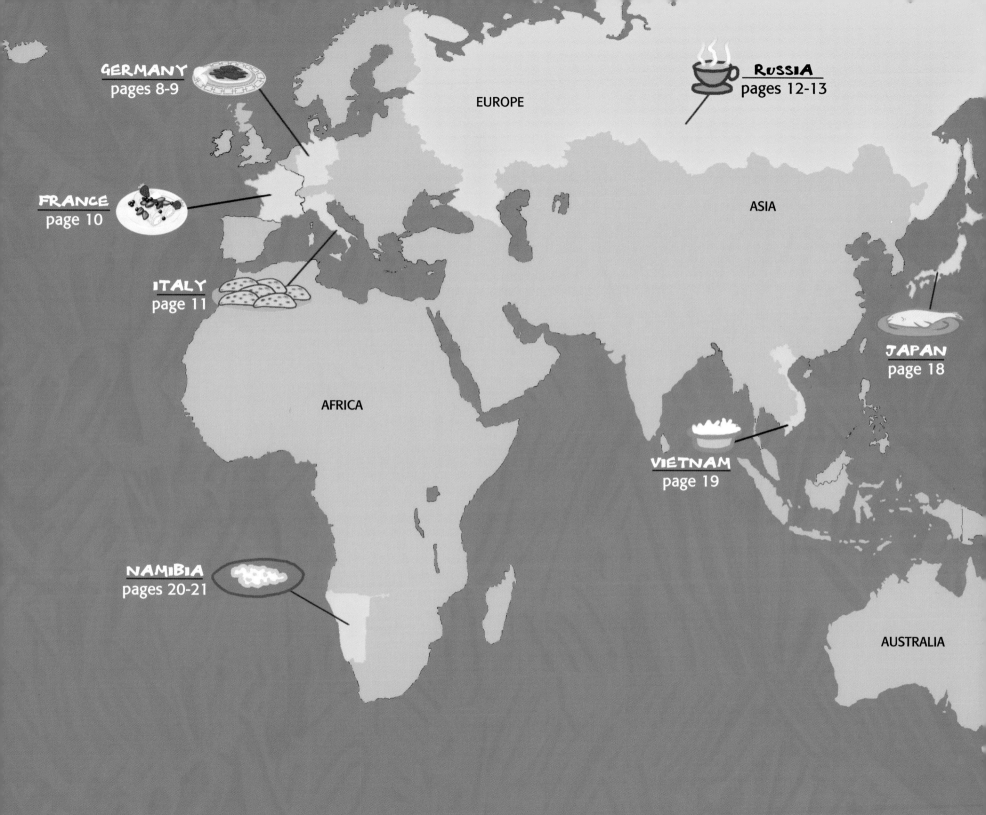

GERMANY
pages 8-9

RUSSIA
pages 12-13

EUROPE

ASIA

FRANCE
page 10

ITALY
page 11

JAPAN
page 18

AFRICA

VIETNAM
page 19

NAMIBIA
pages 20-21

AUSTRALIA

Crunch! Bowls of cereal start the day for children in the United States. Do you like your cereal plain or sugarcoated? Munch on squares, flakes, stars, or tiny doughnuts. Pour milk in your bowl, or eat cereal dry and crunchy right out of the box.

Hot meals are good, too. Eggs and bacon are tasty ways to start the day. Waffles can be covered with sweet, sticky syrup or even thick peanut butter.

HAPPY O's

In Germany, you might find your plate filled with a warm, tasty pancake called a Pfannkuchen (fan-KOOK-khen).

Don't pour syrup on it. Spread fruity jelly on the pancake instead, then sprinkle sugar over the jelly. Lemon slices add extra zing.

sugar

jelly

lemon slices

Some pancakes, called crepes, are as thin as paper. Roll up a crepe, add berries and whipped cream, and you have a favorite French morning meal. Top it off with a cup of creamy hot chocolate. Bon appétit (BONE ah-pay-TEE)!

Cookies make a good dessert for the end of a meal. In Italy, sweet, crispy cookies called biscotti make a great beginning. Coffee is not just for grown-ups. Italian children like to drink caffe latte with their morning biscotti. Caffe latte is hot coffee mixed with milk. Biscotti taste just as good with cool drinks such as milk and orange juice.

Russian children like hot drinks, too. Tea is a popular way to start the day. Add a few drops of milk to make the tea creamy. Children might break off a piece of sweet bread and dip it in the hot drink.

Munchy quesadillas (kay-suh-DEE-uhs) make a morning meal in Mexico. A quesadilla is a thin wheat tortilla stuffed with melted cheese, vegetables, and meat. Now that's a spicy treat!

Mexican children never get tired of the morning meal, because they have so many tastes to choose from. They might enjoy poached eggs and salsa, refried beans, sweet mangoes and bananas, or foaming hot chocolate.

poached eggs and salsa

refried beans

mangoes and bananas

hot chocolate

Gallo pinto (GI-yo PEEN-to) might be your favorite morning meal if you lived in Nicaragua.

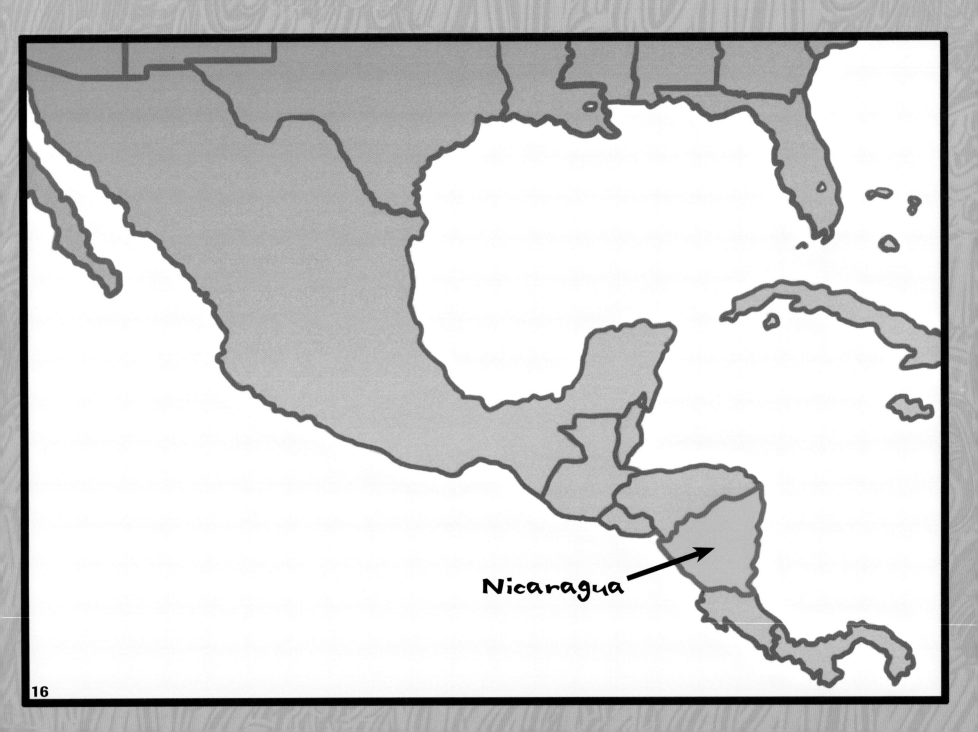

Nicaragua

Gallo pinto is the Spanish name for a colorful rooster. The dish gallo pinto has the same colors as a rooster—two ingredients are bright red beans and white rice. Fried onions, meat, and veggies also can be added to gallo pinto.
The warm, wonderful mixture
is packed into a corn tortilla.

In Japan, each kind of food has its own special bowl or dish. Rice, hot soup, and warm green tea sit side by side on a Japanese table. Add dishes of eggs, crunchy vegetables, or silky tofu to start your morning in a healthy way. And in Japan, any time of day is good for fish.

green tea

rice

soup

chopsticks

fish

Children in Vietnam like their rice good and sticky. They make their morning bowls of rice taste sweet by adding coconut and sugar. Yum!

You could grow your own morning meal if you lived in Namibia. You might raise ostriches for their eggs.

chicken egg

ostrich egg

Scrambled ostrich eggs are a favorite dish. Ostrich eggs
are very large. It would take only one egg to feed your whole family!

All around the world people start the day with morning meals. They might eat something sweet or spicy. They might have refreshing drinks. No matter what they eat, they are getting energy to start the day. What would you like for your morning meal?

Try These Fun Recipes

You Can Make Tea with Milk

Makes 1 serving

What you need: water, a tea bag, milk

What to do:

1. Boil the water. You can boil it in a pan on a stove, or you can place the water in a mug and boil it in a microwave.

2. Place the tea bag in the mug of hot water. Let the tea bag steep in the water for 1 to 2 minutes, then remove the tea bag.

3. Pour a little milk in your tea to make it creamy.

4. When your tea has cooled, you can try this Russian morning treat.

Make sure you have an adult to help you.

You Can Make Mexican Breakfast Quesadillas

Makes 2 servings

What you need:

2 flour tortillas
1 onion
1 jalapeño pepper (optional)
1/2 cup (120 grams) shredded
    cheddar cheese
2 thin slices of ham
1 cup (240 grams) sour cream
1 cup (240 grams) salsa

What to do:

1. Place 1 tortilla on
   a microwave-safe plate.
2. Cut the onion into small pieces.
3. Cut the jalapeño pepper
   (if using) into small pieces.
4. Place the shredded cheese, the
   slices of ham, and the pieces of
   onion (and jalapeño pepper, if
   using), on the tortilla.
5. Cover with another tortilla.
6. Microwave on medium heat
until the cheese has melted.
7. If you like, use any leftover ingredients to decorate your quesadilla.
8. Cut the quesadilla into wedges and serve with sour cream and salsa.

Make sure you have an adult to help you.

Fun Facts

- Many people top their pancakes or waffles with maple syrup. Maple syrup is made from the sap of maple trees. Native Americans were the first to prepare maple syrup. They discovered how to turn the sap into a sweet treat.

- The largest morning meal was served in Taiwan on October 13, 2001. More than 23,000 people ate the meal! Together they drank 1,247 gallons (4,720 liters) of milk and ate 4,232 pounds (1,919 kilograms) of bread. The meal was so big, it had to be served in Chung Shang Stadium.

- In many European countries, the day before Ash Wednesday is known as Pancake Day. On this day, people feast on pancakes and lots of other foods. Pancake Day began because Christians would make pancakes in order to use up butter and eggs—foods they could not eat during the season of Lent.

Glossary

biscotti—crisp Italian cookies

bon appétit—a French expression that means "Enjoy!"

crepe—a very thin, small pancake that is often stuffed and rolled up

Pfannkuchen—a puffy, sweet pancake sprinkled with sugar and served with jelly or fruit sauce

tofu—a soft, cheeselike food. Tofu is made from soybeans.

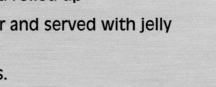

To Learn More

At the Library

Cook, Deanna F. *The Kids' Multicultural Cookbook: Food & Fun Around the World.* Charlotte, Vt.: Williamson Pub. Co., 1995.

Gershator, David. *Bread Is for Eating.* New York: Holt, 1995.

Lauber, Patricia. *What You Never Knew About Fingers, Forks & Chopsticks.* New York: Simon & Schuster Books for Young Readers, 1999.

Morris, Ann. *Bread, Bread, Bread.* New York: Mulberry Books, 1993.

Schuette, Sarah L. *An Alphabet Salad: Fruits and Vegetables from A to Z .* Mankato, Minn.: A+ Books, 2003.

On the Web

Fact Hound offers a safe, fun way to find Web sites related to this book. All of the sites on Fact Hound have been researched by our staff.

1. Visit *www.facthound.com*
2. Type in this special code: 1404802800
3. Click on the FETCH IT button.

Your trusty Fact Hound will fetch the best sites for you!